Eskimos

CONTENTS

© Aladdin Books Ltd

Designed and produced by
Aladdin Books Ltd
70 Old Compton Street
London W1

First published in the
United States in 1984 by
Gloucester Press
387 Park Avenue South
New York NY 10016

ISBN 0-531-03485-2

Library of Congress
Catalog Card No. 84-81106

Certain illustrations have previously appeared in the "Civilization Library"
series published by Gloucester Press

THE CIVILIZATION LIBRARY

Eskimos

JILL HUGHES

Illustrated by
MAURICE WILSON

Consultant
BRIAN LEAS

Gloucester Press
New York · Toronto · 1984

The Eskimo people

The Eskimos live in the cold lands of northern Canada and Greenland, close to the Arctic Circle, which stretch from eastern Russia. The first Eskimo people probably came from Asia many thousands of years ago, possibly walking along a land ridge which is now the Bering Strait.

Until the 20th century the Eskimos continued to live their traditional life, hunting and catching the Arctic animals, birds and fish for food. The same creatures gave them skins, bones and fat for their clothes, weapons and fuel. Little of the animals goes to waste.

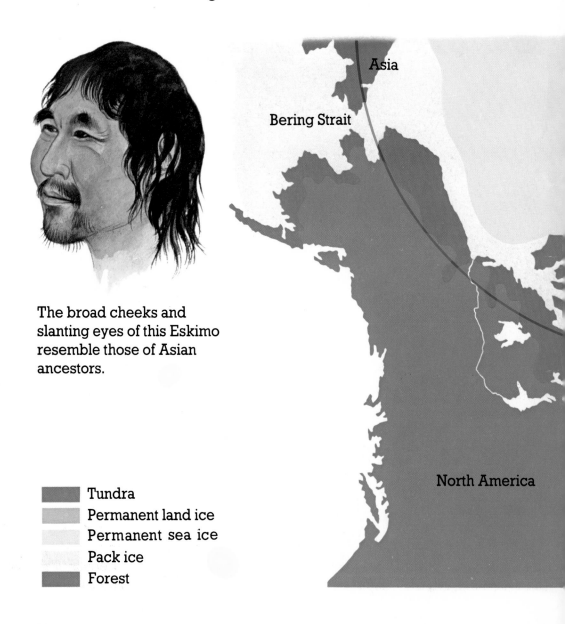

The broad cheeks and slanting eyes of this Eskimo resemble those of Asian ancestors.

Asia

Bering Strait

North America

- ■ Tundra
- ■ Permanent land ice
- Permanent sea ice
- Pack ice
- ■ Forest

The people's land

Although the Eskimos are spread out over a huge area, in most places they speak basically the same language. For a long time they knew no other peoples: their name for themselves, *Inuit*, means "the people." Most Eskimos live on the coasts or north of a line where the forests give way to low-lying land called the tundra. Eskimos live in small groups, relying on each other for help. The old hunting life has gone, but they are the same friendly people today.

Arctic Circle

Greenland

Hudson Bay

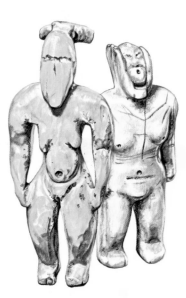

These figures were carved from walrus tusks by people who lived in Greenland almost 3,000 years ago.

Close to nature

The Eskimos are a nomadic people – this means that they move from place to place in search of food. Their Arctic homelands have long, dark winters and short summers when the sun shines for 24 hours a day.

The Eskimos manage their daily lives to fit in with the different seasons. Because they depend on hunting to survive, the Eskimos know all about the habits of animals, and how they are affected by the weather. We have one word for snow; the Eskimos have very many, each describing a different type or state of snow. They must know whether the snow is firm enough for sleigh travel or soft enough to bury traps in. The Eskimos distinguish at least six seasons: early spring, late spring, summer, fall, early winter and later winter. They look at the whole world of Nature much more closely than we do – because their lives depend on it!

Early spring

Late spring

Summer

The Arctic year

In early spring the sky begins to get lighter but the weather is still snowy. Eskimos wait by holes in the ice where seals come up to breathe. The seal provides them with meat, skin clothing and fuel (from its blubber or fat) all year round. By late spring the snow begins to melt. Then the Eskimos move from their winter houses into animal skin tents. In summer they pitch the tents further inland, and hunt the tundra animals and birds, and gather wild berries.

All too soon summer is over. September sees the first snow showers. By October the snow is thick and lakes freeze. Inland, and on the coast, the Eskimos build winter houses. The late winter, with temperatures of $-30°C$, is the darkest and coldest time of year. Only seals or Arctic hare or fox can be hunted.

Fall

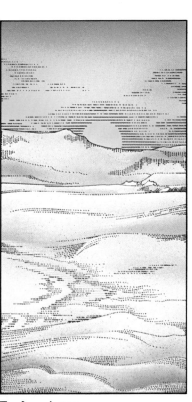

Early winter

Late winter

7

Sea life

In most of the places where the Eskimos live, the sea is a mixture of the Arctic Ocean and the warmer waters of the Atlantic and the Pacific. The coastal seas freeze in winter and spring, but then they make a safe highway for sleigh travel. The Eskimo can cross the ice in search of polar bear, seal and walrus. But in late spring, when the ice is beginning to thaw, it is too dangerous to travel on. Great cracks open up which could swallow a whole dog team. However, with the arrival of summer the seas teem with life. Whales and seals come north from the warm southern waters and millions of sea birds lay their eggs on the cliffs. Several kinds of salmon swarm up the rivers in vast numbers.

Kittiwake

Guillemot

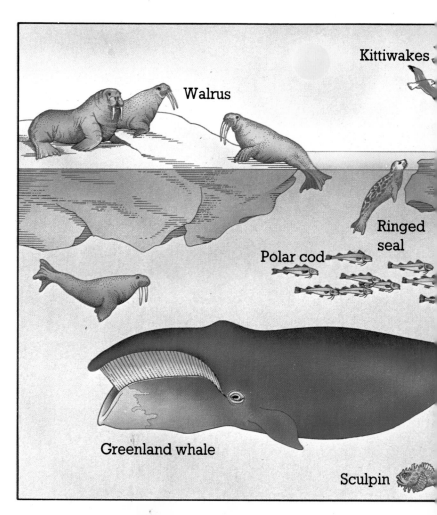

Kittiwakes

Walrus

Ringed seal

Polar cod

Greenland whale

Sculpin

Food from the sea

During the summer season the Eskimos take to their boats to hunt whales, walruses and seals. Besides meat, these sea mammals provide skin and bone. Whale bones are big enough to make the frames of houses and boats. The long single tusk of the narwhal is often carved into beautiful objects. The eggs of birds like gulls, guillemots and kittiwakes can be gathered on the shore. Birds called little auks are shot with bows and arrows. Sometimes hundreds of them are stuffed into a sealskin which is buried under stones. At the end of summer the whole thing, called a *giviak*, is dug up and eaten as a rare delicacy!

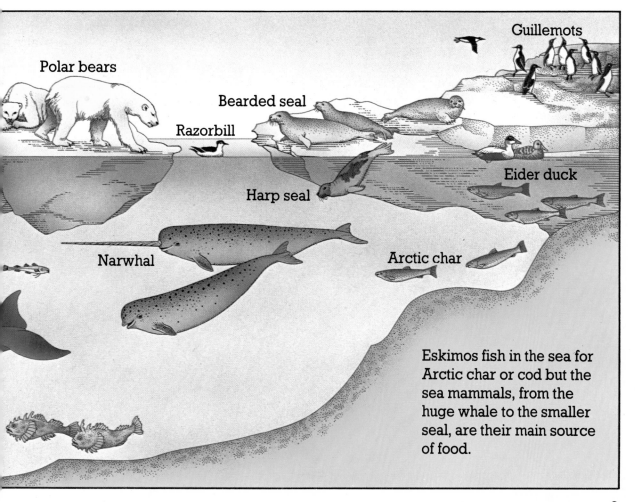

Eskimos fish in the sea for Arctic char or cod but the sea mammals, from the huge whale to the smaller seal, are their main source of food.

Igloos and stone houses

If you asked most people what sort of house an Eskimo lives in, they would reply "an igloo," a snow house. In fact, in the Eskimo language "igloo" means any kind of house. It is used to describe the stone and turf house in the picture below, as well as the seaskin or caribou skin tents of summer. The snow igloos are usually built as temporary winter shelters on hunting expeditions. They are built in the same sort of dome shape as the more permanent stone houses. First the hunters draw a circle in the snow to mark the floor size of their igloo. Then, with an ivory or bone snow knife, they cut the snow "building blocks." These are built up in a spiraling circle until there is a dome with a small hole in the top. This is filled with a single block.

Outside a stone and turf winter house

Inside a snow house

It is surprisingly warm inside an igloo. Heat from blubber lamps and from the people inside makes it possible to go around half naked. The family sleeps on a fur covered platform. Pegs of bone or ivory stuck in the wall above the lamp hold boots, socks and gloves to dry. Wet clothes would not keep out the cold.

Windows

The windows of snow houses are made from thin sheets of ice. For stone and turf houses the Eskimos make windows out of the semi transparent skins of seals' bladders or windpipes sewn together. The one in the picture has a design painted on it.

A sealskin window

The family sleeps together, heads toward the door. The wife is nearest the lamp so that she can refill it if necessary in the night.

A hunter in sealskin parka, trousers and boots (*kamiks*).

Protection against the cold

During cold winters, children sometimes wear parkas, which are called anoraks by the Greenland Eskimos. The original anorak was a hooded jacket of sealskin. In order to survive in freezing temperatures, the Eskimos copy the Arctic animals and make their clothes of skins and furs to keep out wind and wet.

The Eskimos have no cotton or wool. All their clothes are made from skins, fur or feathers. Styles vary from one region to another. In Greenland, women wear costumes gaily decorated with beads traded from white whale hunters. Some Polar Eskimos, men and women, make their inner shirts of bird skins with the feathers worn next to the body. The best way to keep warm is to wear loose clothing in layers. The hunter on the left wears an inner sealskin shirt with the fur side turned in. His loose overshirt, has the fur outside. His sealskin boots are lined with moss.

A Greenland woman in sealskin boots.

A Bering Strait man with an eider duck feather jacket.

An Eskimo woman from Coronation Gulf, Canada.

Travel in the Arctic

In winter the Eskimos move quickly over ice and snow with dog sleighs or on snowshoes. On the coastal waters and inland lakes they use boats. Because wood is scarce in the Arctic, Eskimo boats are usually made of bone frames covered with animal skins. Large boats rowed by several people are called *umiaks*. They are also called "women's boats" because women row them when they are used as cargo boats. The light narrow *kayaks*, paddled by one person, are more like canoes. They are very suitable for seal hunting.

Above is the large *umiak* used for whaling or for carrying cargo. You can see how the *kayak*, right, is made by stretching sealskin over a bone or driftwood frame.

Dog sleighs

The Eskimos themselves find this the most exciting way to travel. Sleighs are made of driftwood, bone or ivory lashed together. The dog teams are well trained. The dogs sleep outside with their tails curled round their noses. The numbers in a team vary from five to fourteen depending on the size of the load, the length of the journey and the amount of food available to feed them. Eskimo women and children look after the puppies until they are old enough to work.

Sleigh runners are covered with soft mud which freezes. Water is then poured over the mud and again freezes, making a slippery surface.

Waste not, want not

Perhaps the single most valuable animal to the Eskimo is the seal. It is hunted in different ways depending on the season. In winter the hunter spends many hours in the bitter cold near holes in the ice waiting for a seal to come up for air. He cuts away snow from a hole with a wooden snow knife and sometimes scratches gently on the ice with a wooden "claw" to attract the seal.

In spring seals can be caught in nets in the sea. In summer, when seals bask in the sun on land, hunters can creep close to the nearsighted creatures to harpoon them. Nearly every bit of a seal can be eaten. As the Eskimos have so few vegetables available they need to eat all of the animal, including the intestines and liver, to obtain essential vitamins in their diet.

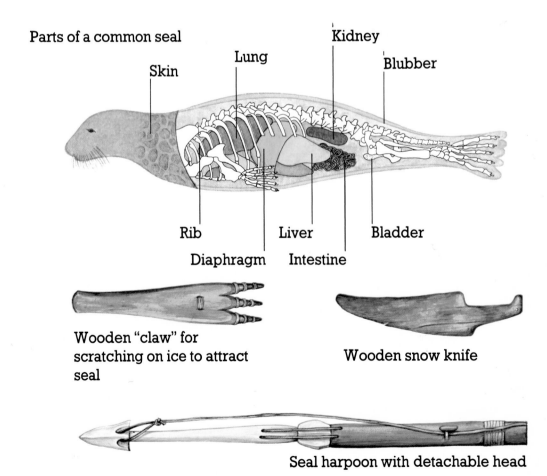

Parts of a common seal

Skin · Lung · Kidney · Blubber · Rib · Diaphragm · Liver · Intestine · Bladder

Wooden "claw" for scratching on ice to attract seal

Wooden snow knife

Seal harpoon with detachable head

Skin and bone

Sealskin is made into clothing and bags and tents. The bones can be carved into knives, needles and other tools. Eskimo women flay the sealskins – this means cutting them away from the carcass and scraping off the blubber or fat. They scrape the insides of the skins first with square ended knives. Then they wash them and peg them out to dry. The skins are scraped again with a curved knife. If the hair is to be removed it is scalded off with boiling water.

The Harp and Bearded seals which visit the Arctic in summer have very tough skins. They are especially good for making ropes and boot soles. Seal sinews are used as thread. The preparation of skins is a job for summer, but most sewing is done during the long winter months.

Women scraping blubber
from sealskins

Whaling

Once the Greenland Eskimos hunted the huge Right whales but these animals are now almost extinct. The Alaskan Eskimos still hunt the Bowhead whale (*agvik*). The Alaskan whaling settlements are larger than other Eskimo groups. Whale hunting depends on precise teamwork and the result can provide food for many mouths. The owners of the *umiaks*, called *umialiks*, are the most important people in their communities.

Inflated sealskins are attached to the harpoons. When the whale is struck, they help to slow it down.

The hunt

The *umiak* crews camp on the ice waiting for the first whale to be sighted. Then the boats are launched, paddled by six men. The harpooners stand in the bows with their 1.5 m (5 ft)-long weapons poised to strike. The whale is slowed down by the lines tied to the detachable heads of the harpoons. The boats all join together to tow a harpooned whale to shore.

A whaling community

The life of a whaling community is a good example of the way in which Eskimos work together to help one another. When a whale has been hauled onto the beach, everyone helps to cut it up. The men cut out the large, pinkish blocks of blubber with "flensing" knives and the women join in to drag them away with big hooks. The blubber is melted to make fuel for heating, lighting and cooking. A thin layer of blubber found close to the skin, called *muktuk*, is eaten as a delicacy.

Cutting up the whale is a social occasion when everyone laughs and chatters excitedly, stuffing bits of raw meat and blubber into their mouths as they work. But the meat is divided up according to strict rules. The crew of the first boat to strike the whale gets the largest share. Everyone has something – even the dogs. Surplus flesh is stored in pits for winter.

Cutting up the whale

Women's work

Eskimo women sometimes help their husands hunt and they know how to drive dog teams and row boats. They can also fish and trap animals. But their most important task is to make warm, windproof clothes for their families, for without these they would die. Women cure skins and cut them economically into shirts and trousers. They sew them with bone needles and sinew thread. They make the skin tents for summer as well.

Women cook for their families, fill the blubber lamps and keep their wicks trimmed, and look after children. When visitors arrive, an Eskimo woman will serve them and her husband before she helps herself. But Eskimo wives are by no means slaves. Like everyone in an Eskimo group, they play their own part in a society in which people help one another.

A woman's circular knife

Women chew skins to make them soft enough to work

A time of plenty

In summer the tundra is alive with plant and animal life. The Eskimos pick cranberries and bilberries. Trout and salmon swim up the rivers from the sea. The Eskimos build dams to trap the migrating fish. Everyone plunges into the water to spear what they can with three pronged harpoons called leisters. Any fish not eaten at once are dried or smoked on racks and kept for the winter.

A last chance

The Eskimos live in caribou skin tents on the tundra. They have a rich summer diet of fish, caribou meat and the wild fruits of the Arctic. When they feel the first chill winds of fall and the ice begins to form on the lakes and streams, they search carefully for the few remaining fish. Using lines, they jiggle model fish in the water as bait and then spear their prey when they rise to the bait. Nets are now used for fishing out at sea – usually for herring.

Summer fishing – the lines in the Eskimos' mouths are for stringing caught fish.

People of the caribou

West of Hudson Bay, in northern Canada, is a great, flat area of land called the Barren Grounds. This is the home of the Caribou Eskimos. They take their name from hunting the huge herds of caribou that stream across the Barren Grounds in fall, moving south to warmer pastures. The caribou are sleek and well-fed after the summer. Their meat and skins, and the tallow or fat for cooking and lighting will last the Eskimos all through the winter. These Eskimos never see the sea. They are totally dependent on the land for food.

Trapping the caribou

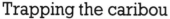

Like whale hunting, caribou trapping depends on teamwork. Several families get together when the herds are expected. The Eskimos know the routes the animals will take. They make models of hunters from stones and peat to head off the caribou to where the real hunters are lying in wait. Then they kill as many as they can with bows and arrows, harpoons, and sometimes rifles.

Stories and songs

The Eskimos are a sociable people who love coming together to sing, dance and tell stories. Many of the stories are about animals who behave, and have feelings, like human beings. The Eskimo language was not written down until recently but these legends were handed down by storytellers. In the fall when there is still food left from summer, and before the winter ice is firm enough to hunt on, the Eskimos have time to relax, often spending hours in "dance houses."

Eskimo carving

The Eskimos make carvings of animals as charms to help them have success in hunting. But they also do honor to the spirits of the creatures on whom their lives depend. Today, carvings of ivory and soapstone are sold to tourists and art galleries as a way of making a living. The best of these carvings are extremely beautiful.

Eskimo drawing of a dance house

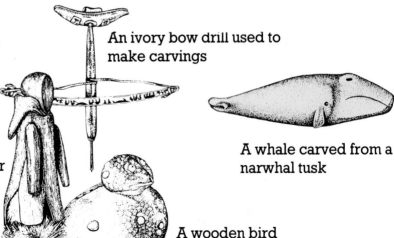

An ivory bow drill used to make carvings

A doll of wood and fur

A whale carved from a narwhal tusk

A wooden bird

Drumming and dancing

All Eskimos love drumming and dancing – the drum is their only musical instrument. It is like a tambourine with a short handle on the rim. Men's dances are dramatic. They act out exciting events from the hunt. Women's dances are gentle and swaying. Men also hold drumming contests. In the past these were used to settle arguments. Instead of fighting, two men took turns to beat their drums and shout out as many insults as they could think of about their opponent!

Ceremonies in the dance houses usually last many hours. The heat inside can be formidable, and people wear as little as possible.

Eskimo childhood

Eskimo parents are very fond of children although they do not spoil them. Children are hardly ever scolded or slapped. From their parents they learn the skills of the true Eskimo, and also to be generous, kindly, and forgiving. Fathers and mothers spend hours carving toys and games for their children.

Games of skill

Two favorite games of Eskimo children are *ajagak* – in which you have to catch a pierced bone plate on a pin – and *nuglutang* – in which several players use pointed darts to try to hit the hole in a piece of ivory.

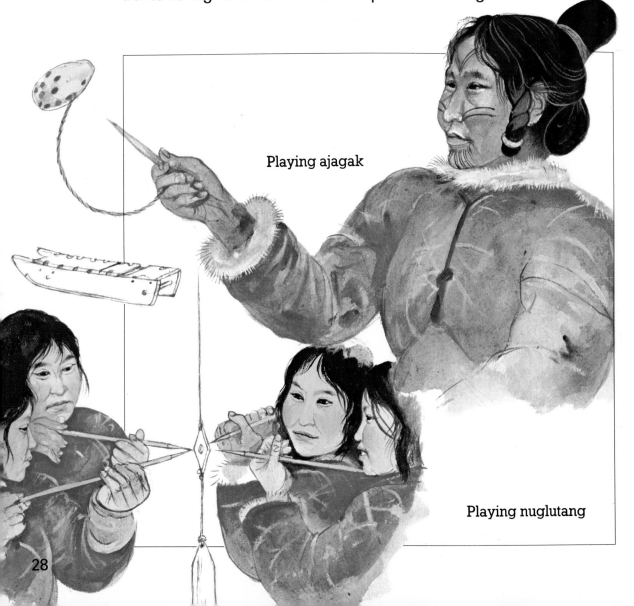

Playing ajagak

Playing nuglutang

Old and young

The childhood games of skill shown opposite help to train the eye and hand as well as being fun. They are useful practice for future hunters. Children also play with toys which are smaller versions of adult things like sleighs and miniature bows and arrows. Children, adults and old people all share a deep attachment to the traditional Eskimo way of life. Old people are particularly respected because they are a link with this tradition. They can teach young people all the skills of hunting and trapping, and making tools and weapons. Today's young people are anxious to revive the old ways.

Only the older Eskimos still remember how to use traditional tools.

A new life for Eskimos?

The old Eskimo way of life that we have seen in the last few pages has almost vanished. Snowmobiles have replaced dog sleighs. Too many animals can be killed by high-powered rifles – harpoons and bows and arrows allowed the Eskimos to kill just enough to feed themselves and preserve the animal population.

Most Eskimos now live in settlements under state laws. Pipelines, airfields and towns are beginning to spread across their old lands. Although they are being paid compensation for oil taken from their territories, the Eskimos are worried about the effect of industry on the local wildlife. Recently an anthropologist – someone whose job it is to study the world's peoples – said, "The hunting societies of the world have been sentenced to death." Can the Eskimos survive the unwanted problems of modern life by reviving the values of the old cooperative, natural life?

Glossary

Agvik Alaskan name for the Bowhead whale.

Blubber The thick layer of fat beneath the skin of a seal or whale.

Flay To strip the skin from an animal's carcass.

Flensing knife A special knife for cutting up whale blubber.

Giviak A tasty dish made by stuffing a sealskin with birds called little auks and allowing the whole thing to mature for several months.

Inuit The Eskimo name for themselves, meaning "the people."

Kamiks Sealskin boots.

Leisters Three pronged fish spears.

Muktuk The thin layer of blubber immediately under a whale's skin which is eaten as a delicacy.

Nomadic Nomadic people have no settled homes but move from place to place in search of food.

Tundra Low-lying grass- and heather-covered land between the tree line and the permanent Arctic ice.

Umiak A large, skincovered boat rowed or paddled by several people.

Index

32

PRINTED IN BELGIUM BY **proost** INTERNATIONAL BOOK PRODUCTION